Landing craft loaded with refugees

# Cornerstones of Freedom

# The Story of
# THE SAIGON AIRLIFT

By Zachary Kent

CHILDRENS PRESS®
CHICAGO

North Vietnamese rockets and artillery shells pounded the Tan Son Nhut air base, halting all flights from the airfield.

Library of Congress Cataloging-in-Publication Data

Kent, Zachary.

  The Story of the Saigon airlift / by Zachary Kent.
      p.    cm. — (Cornerstones of freedom)
    Summary: Describes that dramatic helicopter airlift, the
  largest in history, which during two days in 1975 carried
  thousands of Americans and selected South Vietnamese out
  of Saigon as the North Vietnamese marched to capture the
  city, thus ending the long Vietnam War.
    ISBN 0-516-04760-4
    1. Vietnamese Conflict, 1961-1975 — Vietnam — Ho Chi
  Minh City — Juvenile literature.   2.   Refugees, Political —
  Vietnam — Juvenile literature.   3.   Refugees, Political —
  United States — Juvenile literature.   [1.   Airlift,
  Military — Vietnam.   2.   Vietnamese Conflict, 1961-
  1975 — Aerial operations, American.   3.   Refugees,
  Political — Vietnam.]   I. Title.   II. Series.
  DS559.9.S24K46   1991
  959.704′348 — dc20                                    91-15847
                                                          CIP
                                                           AC

PHOTO CREDITS

AP/Wide World Photos — Cover, 2, 3, 5, 6 (top left and
bottom), 7 (top and bottom left), 8 (3 photos), 9 (top left and
right), 12 (left), 13 (center), 14, 18, 21, 22 (2 photos), 23 (2
photos), 26 (left), 27, 31

Reuters/Bettmann Newsphotos — 28 (left)

UPI/Bettmann — 1, 4, 6 (top right), 7 (bottom right), 9
(bottom), 10 (2 photos), 11, 12 (right), 13 (top and bottom),
15, 16, 20, 24, 25, 26 (right), 28 (right), 29, 32

Cover — Evacuation from Saigon

Page 2  Americans and Vietnamese run for a U.S.
          Marine helicopter during the April 29th
          evacuation of Saigon.

Page 3  Refugees are transferred by landing craft from
          the USS Blue Ridge to a merchant vessel in the
          South China Sea.

Tanks destroyed by the bombing

The sudden blast of a rocket knocked Major General Homer Smith out of his bed at the U.S. Defense Attaché Office (DAO) compound in Saigon, South Vietnam. In the early morning blackness of April 29, 1975, Smith heard the shriek of other rockets crashing onto nearby Tan Son Nhut air base. Scrambling to his feet, he instantly understood the meaning of this surprise attack. The last battle of the long Vietnam War had begun. The Communist North Vietnamese Army had started its final push to conquer South Vietnam's capital city.

Inside the compound, hundreds of Saigon citizens crouched in fear. For days the American soldiers at the DAO had been flying people out of Saigon. By midday of April 29, however, General Smith realized that flights from Tan Son Nhut were no longer possible. The general telephoned his report to

the U.S. Embassy in Saigon and after inspecting the field himself, U.S. Ambassador Graham Martin unhappily agreed. The United States had supported the Republic of South Vietnam for years. Now it was the duty of the United States to get as many Americans and South Vietnamese out of Saigon as possible.

Ambassador Martin telephoned Washington, D.C., and minutes later President Gerald Ford issued new orders for Saigon: Begin Operation Frequent Wind. During the next tense hours an emergency helicopter airlift, the largest ever attempted, carried thousands of people to safety. For the United States the Saigon airlift marked the end of ten frustrating years in South Vietnam. For the escaping South Vietnamese it was the start of an uncertain but hopeful future.

For more than thirty years war had raged throughout Vietnam. In 1941, invading Japanese soldiers interrupted decades of French colonial rule. After the World War II defeat of Japan in 1945, the Vietnamese resented the return of the French to power. In 1946 Vietnamese nationalists attacked French plantations and military outposts. War erupted once more. Eight years later, in 1954, France finally granted Vietnam its independence, but the Vietnamese nation was divided. Democratic nationalists formed a republic in South Vietnam, and Communist leader Ho Chi Minh set up a government in North Vietnam.

Ho Chi Minh

Left: French Premier Pierre Mendès-France and North Vietnam's Foreign Minister Pham Van Dong (at left) represented their governments.
Right: North Vietnamese troops paraded through the streets of Hanoi after the French troops left.

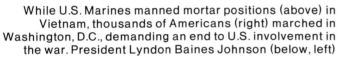

While U.S. Marines manned mortar positions (above) in Vietnam, thousands of Americans (right) marched in Washington, D.C., demanding an end to U.S. involvement in the war. President Lyndon Baines Johnson (below, left)

Grimly, Ho Chi Minh vowed to unite the north and south under Communist control. As early as 1957 Communist guerrilla fighters called Viet Cong began assassinating South Vietnamese leaders. By May, 1965, it seemed clear the South Vietnamese government needed military support. Fearing the spread of Communism, President Lyndon Johnson sent American combat troops into war-torn South Vietnam. Unable to defeat the Viet Cong, President Johnson committed more and more U.S. troops to the struggle. By 1968 more than 500,000 U.S. troops were fighting in the jungles of South Vietnam.

At home millions of Americans bitterly protested

A U.S. soldier (left) stands over the poncho-covered bodies of his comrades. In 1973 a cease-fire agreement was reached (right). Henry Kissinger, across the table, signed for the United States. Le Duc Tho, foreground, signed for North Vietnam. President Richard Nixon (below, right)

U.S. troop involvement in Vietnam. As the war dragged on, it seemed a useless sacrifice of American lives. In time the new administration of President Richard Nixon agreed to reduce U.S. troop involvement in Vietnam. Weary U.S. soldiers gladly clutched their orders shipping them back home. Finally on January 27, 1973, U.S. diplomats signed a cease-fire with the North Vietnamese at Paris peace talks.

About 58,000 Americans had died in Vietnam, but the fighting did not end. The South Vietnamese continued the war, using U.S. supplies. The Army of the Republic of Vietnam (ARVN) fought its Communist

9

Refugees fled down Highway 1 to escape the advancing North Vietnamese troops. Most of them sought safety in Saigon.

enemies for another two years. But, by the spring of 1975, South Vietnam was crumbling.

On March 30, 1975, Communist troops captured Da Nang, South Vietnam's second largest city. By the middle of April, North Vietnamese army divisions attacked Saigon from the north, south, and west. "It's the 25th hour," exclaimed one retreating ARVN officer. "Not even an able leader can rescue the Republic now. It's too late." In downtown Saigon many foreign diplomats closed their embassies and fled the country. The United States, however, was determined to keep its embassy open as long as possible. Several thousand American government officials and private citizens still lived in the city.

10

Day after day, Ambassador Martin and his staff organized the escape of Americans and loyal South Vietnamese. Outside the embassy thousands of South Vietnamese people waved identification papers, offered bribes, and begged for a chance to get out of their collapsing country.

At the U.S. Defense Attaché Office (DAO) near the Tan Son Nhut airfield, Major General Homer Smith and his staff set up daily flights. By April 22, huge C-141 transport planes landed throughout each day, while smaller C-130s touched down at night. In the steaming heat Americans and South Vietnamese clutching passports and luggage crowded aboard these planes. Every half hour another flight rumbled

C-130 transports were used for night flights out of Saigon.

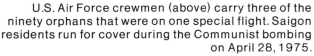

U.S. Air Force crewmen (above) carry three of the ninety orphans that were on one special flight. Saigon residents run for cover during the Communist bombing on April 28, 1975.

down the runways and rose into the sky bound for U.S. military bases in the Philippines and Guam. Some special flights carried only South Vietnamese babies and orphans.

On April 23, 3,824 Vietnamese boarded U.S. transport planes. On April 24, another 5,574 people flew out of Saigon. Many of the escaping Vietnamese wept. They were glad to be free from danger, but sad to think they would never see their country again. On April 27, four Communist rockets smashed into downtown Saigon. Terrified citizens ran through the burning streets as the Viet Cong moved into the outskirts of the city. Another 7,578 refugees flew from Tan Son Nhut that day.

On the following evening five North Vietnamese A-37 Dragonfly jets dropped 500-pound bombs on the Tan Son Nhut runways. The U.S. airlift slowed to a trickle. Only two transport planes left Tan Son Nhut that night.

Then, at four o'clock in the morning of April 29, a screaming barrage of rockets and artillery shells suddenly tore into Tan Son Nhut. Two of the rockets destroyed a guard post manned by U.S. Marines Lance Corporal Darwin L. Judge and Corporal Charles McMahon, Jr. The two marines were killed—the last American ground troops to die in Vietnam.

Across Tan Son Nhut smothering clouds of dust and smoke choked the air. The wreckage of planes and trucks blazed out of control. Landing strips were torn apart or hopelessly blocked. General

Lance Corporal Darwin L. Judge

Corporal Charles McMahon, Jr.

A-37 Dragonfly aircraft flown by North Vietnamese pilots

The charred ruins of a Saigon neighborhood after the bombing

Smith sent word to Ambassador Martin that no more planes could land at Tan Son Nhut.

In Washington, D.C., President Gerald Ford realized that the Communists could not be stopped. It was time to get the last Americans out of the city. At 10:51 A.M. Saigon time, President Ford issued the order to begin Operation Frequent Wind.

This emergency pullout called for the use of helicopters instead of planes. A fleet of forty U.S. warships including five aircraft carriers waited 40 miles off the Vietnamese coast to assist the U.S. withdrawal. On the decks of these warships, U.S. pilots scrambled for their helicopters. At the DAO compound, security guards cut down flag poles and telephone poles. As Viet Cong artillery shells crashed nearby, roaring bulldozers cleared three emergency helicopter landing sites. Then the U.S. radio station at the compound began playing a special tape—Bing Crosby's "I'm Dreaming of a White Christmas." Americans still in Saigon knew this was the secret signal warning them to gather at thirteen evacuation assembly points.

Soon buses driven by American soldiers and embassy officers slowly made their way through streets filled with mobs of frightened Vietnamese. At certain street corners and hotels they stopped to let the waiting Americans cram aboard. Chicago

Two young Vietnamese watch the Americans board evacuation buses.

newspaper correspondent Keyes Beech recalled, "At every stop Vietnamese beat on the doors and windows pleading to be let inside . . . . Every time we opened the door we had to beat and kick them back." Wailing Vietnamese ran beside the buses, terrified at being left behind. When some buses finally reached the DAO gate near Tan Son Nhut, frantic South Vietnamese airport guards fired warning gunshots and shouted, "We want to go too."

At 3:00 P.M., the first wave of whirring CH-53 Sea Stallion helicopters hovered over the DAO compound. As each craft landed, armed U.S. Marines spread out to protect the grounds. Then groups of

Civilians rush to board a helicopter at Tan Son Nhut air base.

frightened evacuees were quickly ushered aboard. The first loaded helicopter lifted off just six minutes after touching down.

"Within little more than an hour," remembered Baltimore newspaper reporter Arnold R. Isaacs, "36 helicopters, each carrying 50 or more passengers, had flown off . . . . My turn came at 3:36 P.M. . . . we were called out . . . and directed toward a helicopter waiting with its rotor whirling on a tennis court, perhaps 200 yards away. 'Run!' someone bellowed, and we galloped over . . . . Breathlessly, we scrambled aboard over the lowered rear loading-hatch. As soon as the last passenger was in, the helicopter bumped along the ground for a few yards and then rose into the air."

The evacuation from the DAO compound continued through the afternoon and evening. At 8:00 P.M. more than 6,000 people—5,000 of them Vietnamese—had been lifted out. By nightfall, helicopter pilots could hardly see through the smoke and the darkness. At 11:30 P.M. a U.S. demolition team blew up secret communications equipment in the main DAO building. Soon afterward, the last marines climbed aboard helicopters and whirled away from the deserted compound.

Meanwhile, the situation at the U.S. Embassy grew much more serious. All afternoon, panicked

Vietnamese had crowded outside the embassy walls seeking help and protection. Buses that were unable to inch through the packed Saigon streets to the air-port began dumping their passengers at the U.S. Embassy. Magazine reporter Wendell S. Merick squeezed through the crowd with newspaperman Keyes Beech but found it nearly impossible to reach the gates.

"Climbing over a barbed-wire barricade," Merick said later, "we tried to get to the main embassy gate but were pushed back by the massed Vietnamese. Our one hope was to get to the back gate, which was likewise blocked by a solid wall of screaming Viet-namese."

Protected by U.S. Marines, civilians board a CH-53 at the U.S. Embassy.

"We were . . . scratching, clawing, pushing ever closer to that wall . . ." remembered Beech. "There was a pair of marines on the wall . . . . One of them looked down at me. 'Help me,' I pleaded. 'Please help me.' He reached down with his long, muscular arm and pulled me up as if I were a helpless child."

Wendell Merick also was pulled to safety. "Never have I been so happy," he later gratefully declared, "as when I fell exhausted inside the embassy compound."

Merick and Beech joined over a thousand people waiting to be evacuated from the embassy. Behind the parking lot in the swimming pool area of the compound, crowds of worried Vietnamese sat amid piles of their belongings. South Vietnamese generals in uniform, the former mayor of Saigon, the city police chief, the fire chief, dozens of Saigon firemen, and hundreds of embassy employees and their families all waited anxiously.

Marine security guards chopped down a large tamarind tree in the embassy courtyard to make room for a landing pad for CH-53 helicopters. "A total not to exceed 100 evacuees had been anticipated from the embassy," Marine General Richard Carey afterward explained. Quickly revised orders were issued to the helicopter pilots flying from the U.S. Navy fleet.

A CH-46 Sea Knight on the embassy's rooftop landing pad

Throughout the late afternoon of April 29, the CH-53 choppers carefully touched down one at a time on the embassy parking lot. Americans and South Vietnamese eagerly scrambled aboard. Other passengers climbed a ladder to reach small CH-46 Sea Knight helicopters that gently landed one after another on the highest part of the embassy roof. At nightfall, a brief rainstorm and the gathering darkness made it harder for helicopters to land. On the ground a clever embassy staff officer set up a slide projector so that a large sharp square of light shone on the parking-lot landing pad.

As they landed, helicopter pilots saw fires and artillery bursts moving toward the city. The North Vietnamese were getting closer. As the minutes ticked past midnight, the airlift reached a crucial phase. In Washington, D.C., President Ford insisted that Ambassador Martin and his staff get out before it was too late. At 1:30 A.M., on April 30, Secretary of State Henry Kissinger called Martin to find out how many people remained in the embassy compound. Off the top of his head, the ambassador guessed, "Seven hundred twenty-six." Anxious Washington planners quickly scheduled just enough helicopter flights to carry that number of people and then shut down Operation Frequent Wind.

Henry Kissinge

The CH-53 Sea Stallions kept landing about every ten minutes. Finally, at 4:20 A.M., the last CH-53 rose from the parking lot and disappeared across the city sky. With deep sadness Ambassador Martin realized that some 400 Vietnamese were still inside the embassy and would have to be left behind. Orders from the White House commanded that the last CH-46 helicopters to land on the embassy rooftop pick up only Ambassador Martin and the remaining Americans.

At 5:00 A.M., the ambassador gravely boarded the next-to-last helicopter. Desperate Vietnamese pounded on the embassy doors and begged not to be left behind. On the rooftop, eleven marines nervously waited for the last CH-46 helicopter. Below, gunshots rang out in the Saigon streets. Rioters smashed store windows and set cars on fire. Just after 7:30 A.M., on April 30, 1975, the final chopper swooped down on the embassy roof. The last marine to scramble aboard carried the embassy's American flag folded under his arm.

Less than three hours later, North Vietnamese Army tanks rumbled through the Saigon streets. One tank smashed through the gate of the South Vietnam presidential palace. By noon, North Vietnamese soldiers waved flags throughout the conquered city. Saigon had fallen. The Vietnam War was over.

U.S. troops (inset) behind their sandbag defenses on the embassy roof protected the evacuees departing in helicopters.

While the victorious North Vietnamese army (left) paraded past the Independence Palace in Saigon, thousands of South Vietnamese families, such as the one shown at right, fled the country.

The Saigon airlift, the largest helicopter airlift ever attempted, had ended. During the frenzied days of April 29 and April 30, a total of 1,376 Americans and 5,595 Vietnamese had been lifted by helicopter out of Saigon. At the same time, the U.S. Navy plucked another 60,000 South Vietnamese from rafts, fishing boats, and cargo ships in the South China Sea. The U.S. government promptly granted permission for as many as 132,000 refugees to enter the United States. A convoy of crowded ships steamed toward U.S. military bases in the Philippines.

Evacuees land at Clark Air Base in the Philippines.

The first Vietnamese refugees jammed into military barracks at Clark Air Base in the Philippines. Another 20,000 refugees crowded into hastily built villages of tents and huts on the islands of Guam and Wake. U.S. officials helped the refugees fill out immigration forms. People lined up for medical exams and doctors gave shots against such diseases as measles and polio. "We're going to get some fine people out of this," predicted L. Dean Brown, head of President Ford's refugee task force. Ragged as they were, many of the first people to escape Vietnam were doctors, lawyers, engineers, and teachers.

Not everyone in the United States welcomed the thousands of new immigrants. In 1975 the U.S. economy was weak and many Americans were unemployed. "We can't be looking 5,000 miles away," complained California Governor Edmund Brown, Jr., "and at the same time neglecting people who live here." President Ford expressed the feelings of most Americans, though, by exclaiming, "They ought to be given an opportunity." Congress swiftly passed the Indochina Migration and Refugee Assistance Act of 1975, which provided money to resettle the newcomers.

After their screening by immigration officials in

Food line at Anderson Air Force Base in Guam

Vietnamese women wait patiently at Camp Pendleton, California (left) and Fort Chaffee, Arkansas (right).

the Philippines, on Guam, and on Wake Island, the Vietnamese refugees streamed into the United States during the first weeks of May 1975. At Camp Pendleton in California, Fort Chaffee in Arkansas, Elgin Air Force Base in Florida, and other military centers, the refugees were welcomed by bands playing patriotic tunes. "We thank all you for this," said Dr. Lam Van Thach to the friendly Americans who greeted his group when they stepped off their plane. "We had to leave our country, all that we have, all that we fought for the past twenty years. We hope the U.S. government will give us a chance to start again our lives, our new lives."

Lam Nguyen teaches English to his Vietnamese students in Arlington, Virginia.

At the U.S. military bases, the refugees received food and clothing. Patiently they waited for sponsors to help them get settled in America. Across the United States charitable agencies, church groups, businesses, and private citizens quickly offered to sponsor needy Vietnamese families. Volunteers taught English classes and found homes for the refugees in every one of the fifty states. The effort to find jobs for these immigrants took longer, but the Vietnamese were willing to work. "Life will be better here," exclaimed one refugee, Maivan Muon. "We don't have to worry about war...any more. I'm willing to wash dishes or be a laborer—anything to get my family settled."

Small boats packed with refugees set sail in the South China Sea. Many boats sank. Some lucky refugees, such as the baby boy at right, were rescued by helicopter.

By the end of 1975, the first 132,000 Vietnamese refugees had found new homes in the United States. Since then hundreds of thousands of other desperate Southeast Asians have escaped their war-torn countries. In leaking little boats, Vietnamese, Cambodians, and Laotians have sailed out to sea. The luckiest of these poor "boat people" have reached such countries as the Philippines, Malaysia, and Singapore. From there most have sought to enter the United States.

The number of Southeast Asians entering

America passed the staggering number of 800,000 by 1990. "Our nation's resettlement of . . . Vietnamese, Laotians, and Cambodians ranks as one of the most dramatic humanitarian efforts in history," declared Roger Winter, director of the United States Committee for Refugees.

Adjusting to life in America is a slow and difficult process for many Vietnamese immigrants. "We are shrubs," explained refugee Tran Van Hung, "planted in a new place, needing care and water to grow again." With the support of family and friends, America's great wave of Vietnamese immigrants

An old Vietnamese man waters the plants in his small vegetable garden in New Orleans, Louisiana.

are determined to succeed. Along the Gulf of Mexico, for example, hardworking Vietnamese fishermen pull in record catches of fish and shrimp. In Massachusetts Luy Nguyen and his family worked one hundred hours a week to save enough money to buy two Vietnamese restaurants. Like the immigrants before them, the Vietnamese gladly have accepted humble jobs. Many have worked their way up to responsible, high-paying positions in the accounting, business, engineering, and science technology industries.

A deep respect for education has helped many Vietnamese. "Learn, learn, learn," Thoa Nguyen tells his children. Youthful Vietnamese take their studies seriously. Year after year bright Vietnamese students win scholarships to American colleges and universities. One proud moment for the Vietnamese community occurred in May 1985 when Cadets Jean Nguyen and Hung Vu graduated from the United States Military Academy at West Point. As young children, both had escaped from Vietnam during the fall of Saigon.

Those Vietnamese who escaped Vietnam at the end of April 1975 will never forget the hope symbolized by the Saigon airlift. For two fearful days American helicopters carried them away from the whirlwind of war. Like so many troubled people

Second Lieutenants Jean Nguyen (left) and Hung Vu (right) were the first Vietnamese to graduate from West Point Academy.

before them, America's Vietnamese now add their chapter to the history of the United States. "We died and were reborn," explained Vietnamese refugee Trung Nguyen; "now we live for each other and for the cause of freedom. Our children's children will call us their American ancestors. I think of that every day."

Frightened Vietnamese orphans begin their long journey to the United States.

## INDEX

## About the Author

   Zachary Kent grew up in Little Falls, New Jersey, and received an English degree from St. Lawrence University. Following college he worked at a New York City literary agency for two years and then launched his writing career. To support himself while writing, he has worked as a taxi driver, a shipping clerk, and a house painter. Mr. Kent has had a lifelong interest in American history. Studying the U.S. presidents was his childhood hobby. His collection of presidential items includes books, pictures, and games, as well as several autographed letters.